ZENO'S ETERNITY

ZENO'S ETERNITY

POEMS

MARK JARMAN

PAUL DRY BOOKS
Philadelphia 2023

First Paul Dry Books Edition, 2023

Paul Dry Books, Inc.
Philadelphia, Pennsylvania
www.pauldrybooks.com

Printed in the United States of America

Library of Congress Control Number: 2022946205

ISBN 978-1-58988-170-9

For Amy

Now and always

give me your hand across the dark
Zbigniew Herbert

Contents

1

2

3

4

5

ZENO'S ETERNITY

1

Memory Song

Day after.
Remembered laughter.

Day before.
Even score.

Day of.
Hand in glove.

Day for night.
Twilight.

Night for day.
Star spray.

Day in. Day out.
Whisper. Shout.

Providence

The beasts say, Eat me . . . The trees say, Pull me.
  George Herbert

The virus says breed me.
                    The head says cradle me.
The cancer says braid me.
                    The heart says ladle me.
The star says wish on me.
                    The ocean says plumb me.
The moon says wash me.
                    The plum says preserve me.
The poem says read me.
                    The fat says store me.
The pome says seed me.
                    The feat says perform me.
The word says utter me.
                    The menace says fear me.
The udder says milk me.
                    The fare says pay me.
The past says remember me.
                    The sky says cloud me.
The post says hang from me.
                    The air says clear me.
The soul says save me.
                    And sole says only me.

With Marcus Aurelius in Los Angeles

I have taken a seat in a garden of open sky,
hedged with ficus and bougainvillea,
the bristling red flowers of bottlebrush,
and a couple of lemon and lime trees
from one of many forgotten orchards.
The December sunlight, mellow and gaudy,
leaning west, is slanting in, like truth,
pushing the winter chill into the shadows.
And the truth is I am sitting nearly paralyzed
in an aftermath of despair, having returned
to the place I think of as home and expecting
the end of the world, my life, our country's life,
as I scratch words into the notebook on my lap
where I also balance the book you called, *To Myself.*
I am here, Marcus Aurelius, with your thoughts,
each as stony as a eucalyptus pod in leafy rubble
at the base of a tree too grand for this place.
"Nature always has an end in view," you wrote.
"My city is the Cosmos," you wrote.
A mile or so away a famous boardwalk
skirts the gray Pacific, and ragged souls there
find a way to eat by selling painted sea shells and pebbles,
and in the open air markets, tourists probe
racks of t-shirts and hats with palms and clouds.
The homeless make their homes on the hard sand
and the languages of the empire ripple past.
And even nearer the same babble of humanity
runs along an expensive shoppers' street
where there is not a single necessary thing for sale.
If we accept that one day the sea will cover us

or retreat from us completely, abandoning the earth,
and that it may be tomorrow or the day after, even
as we hear the rumbling surf rise an octave
or note an unusual silence in the silence we are used to,
who knows what the sea will do to this city like a sea?
The garden shadows are crossing the pages
of my notebook while your pages remain sunlit.
Nature always has an end in view—for us
if not for itself. Our gift is to see that.
Our nature is to see and not wholly believe.
Marcus Aurelius, philosopher,
one of the five good emperors of Rome,
I won't pretend you were other than a dictator,
who squandered his reign in looking after his own soul.
"A little flesh, a little breath," you wrote.
"And a reason to rule all that is myself."
You lived at the end of a fortunate era,
says a historian who loved you, and still urged
yourself to rise daily and do the work of a human being,
to stop philosophizing about what a good person is
and be one.

December 2016

The Conversion of the Vikings

One year they're killing monks on eye-white beaches.
The next they're setting up as lifeguards there.
One year they plunder reliquary jewels.
The next they're building churches for their plunder.

What made them all repent? Some kind of magic
that filled their sails or cured a fevered child.
A spell that may have risen from that blood
they spilled on beaches of crushed cockle shells.

And now they burrow in like cuttlefish,
wanting to be left alone by seawrack
and all those portents that they used to live by,
kill by, too. They met the faith of islands.

And it seduced them. They seduced themselves
with silhouettes of landfall, pale blue accidents,
each promising a place to take and hold
for the world's untethered traveling murderers.

The Dancing Satyr

I have been dancing 2000 feet deep,
dancing too for as many years,
a figure of ecstasy, rapture of the deep.

I sent up a limb in a fisherman's net,
then toiled the same way up to join it.
I have been dancing 2000 feet deep.

Frozen from birth in my bronze flesh,
I was born to dance and be motionless,
born into ecstasy and the rapturous deep.

I sank with head thrown back, spine bowed,
with mother-of-pearl in my unclosed eyes.
I have been dancing 2000 feet deep.

And those members I have parted from,
right leg, arcing tail, both arms,
still figure in ecstasy, rapt in the deep.

Whether on the sea floor in the dark
or bathed in lights in my own museum,
still I am dancing centuries deep,
a rapture of bronze and ecstatic sleep.

Mazara del Vallo

A Swan from Prague

I was making my way in half-steps across a bridge
in that city of bridges, and met coming my way,

looking head-on like a fat white ham with wings,
a swan in flight, waist high, at the bridge crest.

I was inching along as the swan with its yard-long neck
towed its floating midriff in air speeding past.

Lost, it wanted back to the city's river,
a river with two names in opposing tongues.

I looked ahead and saw some police laughing
at the wings going mad and the paddle-feet tucked.

I could not remember not being in pain,
not being a man with bone spurs gouging his hip.

In that city of memorials, among memorials
of immolation and metamorphosis,

I thought about this place in history—
the tanks and altered road signs from '68,

the thugs roaming through videos of '89—
and knew for this span of time there was no place.

The police saw me leaning and halting
and turned to watch the swan, as I did,

all of us grateful to be distracted.
And I was sure that they, the laughing police,

imagined that whatever my trouble was—drunkenness,
disability—it would take care of itself,

and that the bird would come to rest again
on the river, the river of clashing names.

I told my wife this story, and as a memento
she gave me a solid bubble of Czech crystal,

a lovely blue-headed swan which rides
now on a shifting river of paper.

Almost

Almost grasped what Grandmother Grace knew
last Sunday sitting in church, almost knew
what Alexander Campbell grasped when, confronted
with the desolate orphan, he told her, "You
are a child of God. Go claim your inheritance."
Almost got it. There it was in the sunlight,
squared in the clear glass windows, on the durable leaves
of the magnolia outside. Almost grasped the weather
that turns clear and crystallized in Hans Küng's brain.

Almost held it in the ellipses and measure
of my almost understanding. I see the moment
there in my notebook, then the next day's anxiety
spilling like something wet across the ink.

I almost put in my hand a vast acceptance
and almost blessed myself, then it slipped away.
All that colossal animal vivacity—smoke
of the distant horizon, most of it, haze.
But to have known in any place or time
what *they* knew is worth a record, a few notes.
Almost knew what they knew. Almost got it.

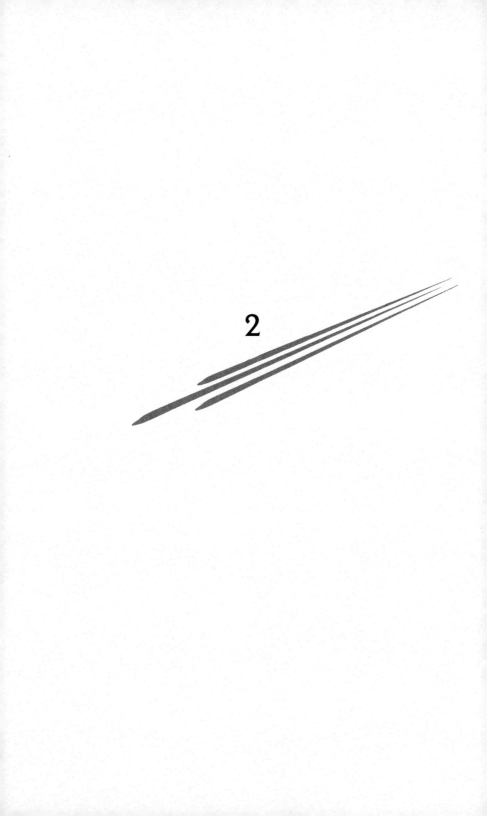

2

The Arrow Paradox

Zeno sent
his arrow flying
endlessly from point
to point along its arc
to make a point
about eternity:
getting there is tricky.

That's what I think
anyway, snowflakes
stalled in the morning's
freezing air
like seed fluff
reluctant to drop
anchor in the ice.

I'm watching that
tentative descent
though I'm in motion
and counter motion
even as I follow
my pen's blue notes
and think I'm not—

not doing anything,
not going anywhere
much farther
than my own flight
across the blank
momentum
of the turning page.

Cause Me to Hear

"Cause me to hear
thy lovingkindness
in the morning,"
in my bedfellow's voice,
in bird whistle, downpour,
in stirring and yawning,
under the overpass,
near the air force base,
in the classic ring tones
rippling the quiet
in the flood and rubble zones
where bodies still breathe,
as your lovingkindness
in the morning in the night
answers the calling
of the rescue team.

Psalm 143

Come Away, Come Away

After the massacre, to make love,
to lie on the morning paper, after the massacre
and after making love, and sing together
a song of Shakespeare's.

After the horoscopes and the massacre,
to express our own defiance
and come away from death inoculated
for a day of dread.

To read the paper and to ask each other
what mourning to wear,
sitting side by side in bed, gazing
into the future.

Then turning to each other and to nakedness,
alive—alive in all likelihood for a long time,
more than long enough to make love,
to sing, after the massacre.

This Is the Day the Lord Has Made

This is the day the Lord has made,
   this is the hour, this is the minute,
     this is the second the Lord has made
ticking.

And after the second, this is the third,
   the fourth, the fifth, squared and cubed,
     this is the finite and the infinite
colliding.

This is the mind in self-regard,
   staggered, speechless, almost amused,
     to see the day the Lord has made
unmaking.

But not too quickly or too slowly,
   just fast enough, all things being equal,
     and fair enough to excuse oneself
for living.

Our Life

Our life is daily happiness together
and nightly sleep or restlessness
and knowing that the other is
awake or dreaming.

All that follows with the sun
or happens in the phases of the moon
or draws its meaning from the zodiac
is part of it—

The all of larger alls and smaller ones,
the borders that are drawn, made like a bed,
set like a table, the loving views,
close or from a distance.

We have our daily life, our only life,
but just as close as we can make ourselves
there has to be at least a little distance
we can cross.

Galaxy

O world flung inward by an arm of stars,
feeling out of control or stalled,
O friend or enemy, propelled
always it seems without effort—

O make a joyful noise,
you're on your way,
your transit has been noted
and made music.

Growing Rain

Term my parents learned in a church of farmers,
in eastern Kentucky, the place where I was born,

and said the rest of their lives, in Scottish mist
with a tang of coal smoke, and in Oregon overcast.

A growing rain, they said, whenever it fell
gently and steadily, soaking without beating down,

even on Christmas Day on patchy snow,
a growing rain, though mealy, thin, or pointless.

Good shoes darkened side by side at the bus stop.
Woolen coats hung down with water weight.

Crowding drops bled together on the windshield,
enriched the pavement. More than enough for all.

The surplus of good and evil saturated
the daily news and, reaching from its cloud

on the X-ray, the cancer quietly budded, blossomed.
The growing rain kept falling all their lives.

Seam

The pain can be endured until it can't.
  The therapy will work until it won't.
The light will fill the room until it's out.
  The kisses halt, or should, when one says, "Don't!"
And sleep will come as long as you can wait.
  The weavers—bird and spider, human being—
are born to knot and net, a kind of fate.
  And every seamless garment has a seam.
Where no horizon's visible the dawn
  breaks out like a flash mob, ready or not.
Better to let it help you put your clothes on
  than hide them in a deeper, darker spot.
A clear blue sky can load the atmosphere
  and laughter greet the weight of a monsoon.
Childhood can end abruptly or stay here,
  looking for those who left to come back soon.

MARK JARMAN

Seminar on "The Purloined Letter"

Days or light years ahead,
as Jacques Lacan has said,
a letter always arrives
at its destination.
Even a dead letter,
a message in dimpled clay,
its data fossilized,
arrives, all the better
for us to crack its codes—
news from the front,
fresh odes,
old news from lover to lover.
Folded in wave or particle,
envelope, riverbed,
a letter arrives, is always arriving
at its fate—to be read or unread.

Hillwood

That winter we could hear the hillside breathing
below our bedroom window every night,
a heavy shaggy exhale with no inhale
as if a thing were breathing from its roots
and came to breathe the night away against
the outer clapboards, where in summer, wasps
hovered with dangling grass stem cargos to lodge.
It wasn't a hive's mind at work, but I'm not sure,
and it was winter and the hill leaned like a bear
and huffed, that's right, huffed against the wall
right underneath our bedroom window until dawn.
We stopped noticing until it also stopped.
And there were nights when we turned out our lights
when the breathing did not start again; we waited
and fell asleep to each other's resting breathing.
Too big to be a raccoon or a possum, but not
to be a doe in a safe place among the japonica.
And I have thought perhaps it was a sign
the mind gives of what's to come in dreams,
this being a kind of vigilance. When it was gone,
we missed it but soon stopped missing or giving it
shape, that bear which never showed itself by day,
that coyote or pregnant doe or exhausted vagrant,
creatures of the night, so imaginable
that you wouldn't want to find out what they were,
depriving you forever afterwards
of that peace of mind you need when you drop off.

MARK JARMAN

She Twirled Along the Brick Wall, Fingertips

She twirled along the brick wall, fingertips
clawing at mortar to take hold
and skittering over the wall face like a keyboard,
frantic, muted.

And I as usual was just trudging along,
head down—on ice this time—more of a mincing
than true trudging, though my soul trudged,
when I caught her.

Slim, young, padded in pleated fleece,
and taller than I as I helped her stand,
she pulled an earplug out beneath her knit cap,
said, "Ouch."

And said it like a quiet bid for privacy.
Paternal, winded, I wanted an assurance.
And she assured me with a thanks that meant,
"Just let me cry."

Sick Fox

News is not good for foxes on our hillside.
Mange is taking all the newborn kits.
And out for a walk around the neighborhood,
late afternoon, late spring, sky muddy gray—
I saw a grown fox lurch from a laurel thicket
and waver in the middle of the road
that slopes down half a mile to the highway.
I watched her—was she a she?—stagger, stop,
chew at a bald spot on her patchy fur,
fold her legs up oddly, one by one,
and sink down near the white dividing line.
It must have been the illness I was looking at.

She lifted up her head when I came closer
and put it down again. The news is not good.
It must have been that, that I was looking at.
And grief. I was looking at grief.

Brink

Now evening pauses on its way toward night.
And through the trees and their uncertain green,
the sky appears in gaps and distances,
pale windows cut into a web of shadow.

It's cool now. But tomorrow who can say?
A rose-breasted grosbeak sat at the feeder today
shelling sunflower seeds neatly as it chewed,
in no hurry to return to Canada.

All the birds have turned invisible now,
though audible signs of them keep wavering.
Wednesday night praise music travels
from the red-brick church across the hollow.

Now bats—the little brown bats—flit back and forth
like nurses without lamps. And souls pass
among the other migrators on their way.
My father's, too, departing on his 89th birthday.

Now That the Father's Gone

the sons are equal,
the daughters, too—no one is number one.

Each will step forward with a eulogy
and sing the survivor's song.

That song includes nothing from the nest,
nothing that used to out-scream other songs.

It will not gape to be fed first or wing-push
the others out.

The song—if anyone can truly sing it—
has never aimed at eloquence or soared

but pivots from the stage, laconic, humbled,
after a word.

There is no one among the favored children
who can achieve the parent's range of song.

And that is what each sings—that falling short
is the survivor's song.

MARK JARMAN

One of Us, Waiting

Chemo wrenched her aching back,
robbed her sense of smell.
She can't get comfortable, eat well.
Except for pomegranate juice,
one thing she can taste.
She lives on it. If she could
right now she'd drink a glass.

X-ray will tell her what she knows.
Spine's a cracked whip. After this
she'll have more than a sip
of pomegranate juice
from those tangy purple capsules.
And one day she'll hang up
her cane, on hell.

End of the Day. Knifing Wind.

End of the day. Knifing wind.
Slanting twilight like melon rind.
Prickling sleet. Brisk afterglow.
To go home or not to go.

And morning then. Taste on the tongue
of last night's thirst, a dream sprung
like a tricky murderer from jail.
A spray of sunshine. Gunshot hail.

The night between. After the day,
at either end, a mind astray
among bare crowns and roots of trees,
touching the raw extremities.

End of dawn. And the night's end,
with headlights sweeping around the bend,
catching one afraid to balk
with deer blind eyes and forward walk.

No One Understood the Final Meal

No one understood the final meal,
that it was final, each part with a meaning.
No one understood, as it was served—
each portion of the body poured, doled out.

Strange flesh. Strange drink.
Each portion of his body.
And as they ate and drank, he talked,
even had a private conversation.

All they remembered was eating with their friend,
a meal they'd had so many times
and known the order of. What was the order?
But who can remember dinner yesterday?

Forgiven for a crime not yet committed,
enjoined to remember someone not yet lost,
they tried to bring them back—
the taste and texture, somehow, the meal, him.

Blackout Good Friday Night

Blackout Good Friday night,
wind and sizzling dusk
crackling and draining,
no light.

Saplings lopped off,
old trees toppled
on the ragged
mandala of their roots.

The friends of Jesus in their grief pit
had no idea that they were only waiting.
The dawn was rising
underfoot.

Living by candlelight, cursing the darkness,
we are not lost but only waiting,
already fast asleep when the lights
come back on blazing.

Our Inconstant Moon

is constantly returning,
maculate, immaculate,
old and new.

Isn't she lovely?
Isn't she scary?

A cipher at the start,
she rounds, lopsided,
tooling across the ecliptic,
one of the powers.

Night is with her
even in the daylight.

A ghost by morning
with blue sky in her craters,
she is like that dream
we almost remember.

The thick sun blares.

But when we see the moon
a hand extends,
speckled with age
and stronger than it looks

The answer? She's scary.
The answer? She's lovely.

At dawn the inner chatter
risen to a howl
scatters into birdsong.

Her note pinned
just at the horizon
reminds us
that she watched us
while we slept.

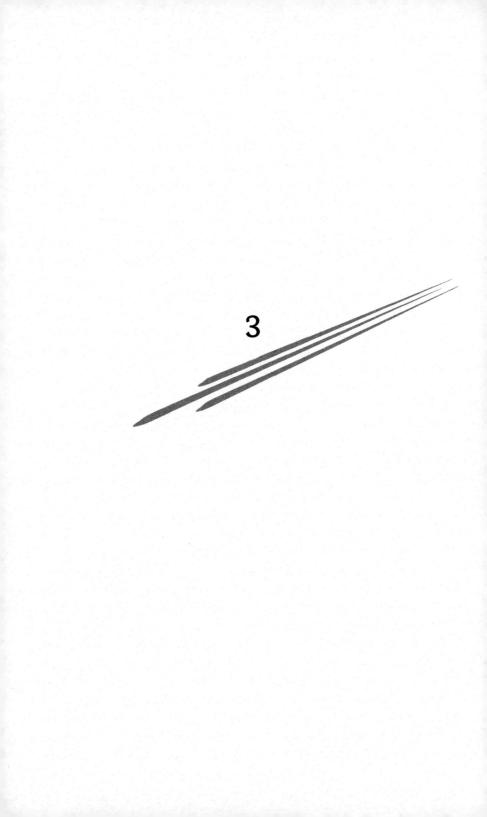

3

Altarpiece, Three for Dante

1. This Place

—First fall day, the first real day of fall,
and there will be another after that.

—Firm footing gave the maker of the world
to man and woman, once they settled down.
Almost at once ground shifted underfoot.

—This place is not so bad. It's not so bad.
We rode here on the eon and the instant
and probability's our one clairvoyance.

—Why do we feel so lost among these trees?

—Don't think about it but let muscle memory
ease the descent. The occasion's gravity
appears in green grime under fingernails
and scales the damage done by sun to scalp.

—Where were we? Oh, once upon a time,
gray drizzling overcast, bright yellow gingkos,
the first day that was purely an autumn day,
and in tomorrow's forecast, brilliant sunshine
like a folktale forestalling ugly death.

—But we're not gonna die tomorrow yet.
We'll wait to see the peak of fading color.

—How honest can it be to remain sane?

—They only lasted six hours in the garden.

2. The Other Place

Down where the murderer and thief,
the liar, the ruiner of childhood,
the sinner who's a cutthroat from the womb,
the banger, bomber, roller out of hangars—
hang out, it's all a lot more colorful.
Up here the mountain sides you have to cling to,
monochrome and sheer, too close for comfort,
keep you focused on getting on with it.

Take envy, Good Lord! It's already painful,
wanting this one's heart, that one's rifle scope,
this one's loving viewpoint, that one's book review,
like trying to fill a trophy room with dog doo.
With both eyes woven shut, all you can see
is the lining of your skull's own nooks and crannies.

Apparently a purging makes you lighter,
though I have heard the bitter aftertaste
turns down the corners of your mouth forever,
and burning off the fat can waste your heart.
Wanting to have that boyish girlish figure,
eating and gagging up the dog's dinner,
will help you let it out and make it better.

But in the other place no one gets better.

3. That Place

At last, at last, up here you can be good,
and over there and under, all around,
the way you always wanted but forgot.
And yet and yet desire still exists.
Not everybody's looking up at God,
that waterlily in the pond of heaven.
Some shimmy and some shine, and some cavort,
enjoying one another bathed in grace.
The argument is amazingly familiar:
if nature were allowed to take its course
and it was understood, its basic goodness
would fit us in the element made for us,
if only we would do what we were told,
not by our parents, who probably didn't listen,
but by our hearts and minds and willing members
as easily as touching a finger to your nose.
Some may enjoy more radiance than others
but everybody gets the same sunshine,
apportioned to the genius of their skill.
That one that you were always meant to be,
dogeared or foxed or sun bleached on a shelf,
will bind you, soul and body, to yourself.

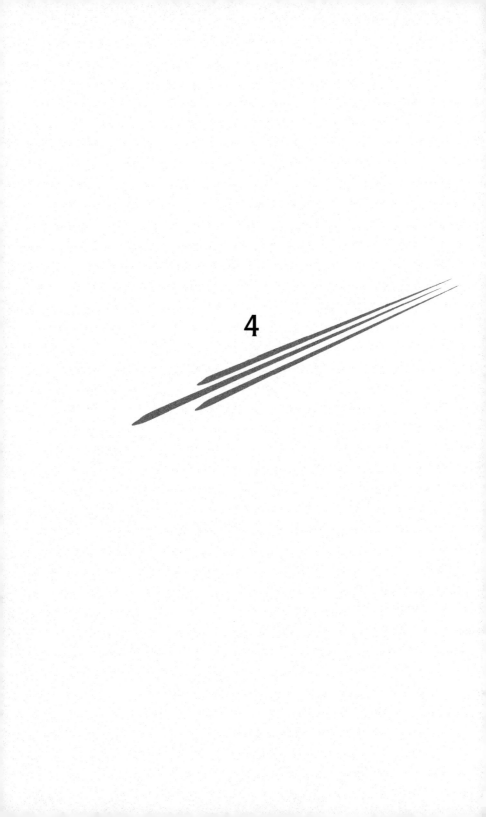

4

Near Cape Lookout

So we kept looking and found a little space
   spangled with fog-milk, drooping asters,
and coiled bending ferns, a sodden enclosure.
   No path there, but a steep unfriendly view
of water far below and hard damp beach.
   Not the place for Mother that we'd hoped to find,
but a woven shrine of wetness and hidden grasses.
   We did find our way down, the waves spread in,
we scattered her from a tea cup she had saved.
   And that bower, with its dewy microclimate?
For all our stumbling in and stopping there
   it may have been like a memory she'd kept
and never told, never told anyone,
   of life before us, before any of us.

Yahrzeit

1

This was the woman who remembered her childhood.
This was the woman with a girl's voice.
This was the woman who recoiled from cameras.
This was the beauty who hated her pictures.
This was the woman who loved dining out with her children.
This was the woman her grandchildren knew as a ghost.
This was the woman who bore no resemblance to herself.
This was the woman who slipped away. We watched as she
    passed out of sight.
This was the woman who gave us no clue.
This was the woman who never lost her sense of humor.
How could she have held on to laughter and nothing else?
This was the woman lost for so long we could hardly remember her.
This was the woman our spouses recalled as ebullient, full of
    laughter, up for anything.
This was the woman who for days after she died came back to me
    in images of her anger.
This was the woman whose leave-taking was long and exit abrupt.

2

She was unconscious but listening.
She was unresponsive but responded.
She lay in the room where the doctor spoke to us.
She lay unconscious, unresponsive, preparing her response.
She did not wait while we left to make arrangements.
She did not wait while we walked out to the front desk.
She must have heard, we told ourselves later.

She must have decided, we assured ourselves later.
This was the woman who lay unconscious and listening.
This was the woman who lay in her bed and left.
She left before we could return to see her off.
She had loved our visits, we believed, and hated saying goodbye.

3

My earliest memory of her is of standing in the doorway
of the bathroom as steam poured out around us,
and I saw her coming forward, naked, annoyed
that I had interrupted her shower. She is there
in a body I have never forgotten, leaning toward me
and telling me to go to my room. The body she left us.
I must have been three or four. I could see the blank cesarean scar
where my sisters and I emerged. Fifty years later,
dressing her after her surgery, I would see her body again.
Young and old at once. No change but difference.

4

On her stone we have written
On her stone we have depicted
We have etched on her stone
Engraved on her stone
Unveiled her stone reads
Her dates on her stone are
We have spelled her name
We have agreed that the stone should say
We have agreed to unveil
The empty air

The Children's Zoo

The Poet's Word

You know the wild person you do not meet,
but flails her arms ahead of you in a store
and heads out to the parking lot, where her car
is dangerously placed near yours. She careens
out of her space, and you—careful, resentful—
pause and let her drive away, far away—
always on the lookout for her frenzy
or his frenzy (let's be fair), and give him
a preoccupation, like pride, in the form of a panatela
and the wide rear end of a Continental.
Always alert, these you must let go ahead
or, if you risk it, you must pass—
anything to be clear of their heedlessness—
and yet, shaking your head in superiority
can turn to choking with rage: they are the forces
that all the organized world keeps in check
for your sake, by your careful planning; ready
to cave in, cross the line, to turn on you.

The Son's Word

That's what we were like at the children's zoo
where we lost the kids. If I name them both,
and name the two of us, will I have fiction
or the strange afictional world of the poem?
But does it matter with an anecdote like this?
Two adults had two children and we lost them.
Dad pushed the gate wide with one hand and asked,

"Are they with you?" My children is who he meant—
the little girls. Then, when he heard my answer,
"No? Where?"—he let the gate shut. And his son, me,
stupid with dread but also officiousness,
stood outside the exit, waiting. People came out,
summery tourists, their children, I peeked in.
I didn't want to pay or violate
the decorum of paying; it didn't take long
for me to damn my own host of ceremonies
(more on them later). Inside the children's zoo
was quieter, even cooler, than the semi-tropical
traffic and softening tar of the zoo at large.
Beyond this scaled-down compound the peacocks cried
for help, and it was then my father, lumbering toward me,
bellowed the children's names, and, "Help!"
came the peacocks in counterpoint, as nearby
a bank of children and adults watched a parrot
speak and feed, its blue cashew shaped tongue
protrude and withdraw. Then a house of mirth,
where children smeared plexiglass with their smiles,
the petting zoo of patient goats and turtles.
A baby elephant snatched a peanut sack
from a startled little fat boy who cried out.
"What happened?" "I left them *here*," my father said
and pointed to a bench. "And told them to wait
while I went in *there*"—the Men's Room, a lion's mane—
"When I came out they were gone." Now, my father
was tall and stout, though gravity and failure
had rounded him downward, he looked down
at me his son who wanted to shriek outrage in his face,
but—but pursed my lips and flew into silent panic.
Sent now to the feeding labs, where the meals were mixed
and lost children kept. A teenager there in uniform

tried to calm me. Now, in a frenzy to the main gate,
my father still staggering along the petting zoo,
calling with the peacocks, attended by guards
who were children, watched or not watched,
regarded by the rectangular pupils of goats,
the dangling semi-wet snout of the elephant,
the turtles introspective and softhearted.

The Father's Word

The older man turned to a child guide, or guide of children,
and said, "My son's twice as angry for their sake
and for another reason. They're here somewhere—
and he knows it. It's his mother." The guide looked
as if for somebody else to count as missing.
"I left her a year ago. That's why he's angry.
He'll find them soon enough. I told them to wait
here, so let's sit now and wait. I understand
he'd like to blame more on me than this—
because he's going to find the little girls,
weep and accuse them, but his mother and I
will never be united in this world.
Too much that can't be taken back gets said—
(Your parents are divorced? But you don't recall?
That's like never knowing them, I'd guess. I'm sorry.)
It would be like a snake slipping on its skin again
and having to match the geometry exactly
to totally forgive, and who would start?
You're not who you were after 30 years,
and she's not either. We got to be like those turtles.
Everything so slow and so hardened into a pattern,
we only sort of rubbed each other passing
with the crumbling edge, not the sensitive part.

Oh, she was shocked, and I was, too, when I said
no more and left the counselor's office. In the car
I'd asked myself what I'd done, and yet
I felt alive, bared and effervescent,
and thin-skinned—all heaviness was gone.
No, I'm not forgiven, but here to see the children.
not him, really, and yet there was a truce.
I've curled my hair, bought a red car, and
have no right to fun, he thinks, because I broke her heart.
Look there they are. I knew it. In the ticket booth!
Thank you, young lady. We'll be all right now.
You ought to hire more help, though. I noticed
nobody was overseeing the petting zoo.
Those poor goats must take a lot of punishment.
Yes, they've all been crying. I can see."

In the First Minute Without Him

In the first minute without him, I felt love
for what he left behind, though it was empty,
and kissed his forehead, and knew it would dissolve
with all the rest in fire and memory.

The last word he said to me was "water,"
repeated three times, and I made a joke
about what Christ got for his thirst—vinegar—
I put the wet sponge to his lips and stroked.

"Water" had been his last word. And his first?
No one is alive who might remember it.
All dying may be a process of growing thirst.
He beckoned with a curled finger at his mouth.

I felt love and said to him, "We loved you."
Corrected myself and said it in present tense.
He believed love transcended death or used to.
He believed love was an extrasensory sense.

Meanwhile where was he, if not lying there,
still present, such a presence we all said,
his tall man's length and breadth, his preacher's pompadour,
his daily need to tell the world he lived.

Our father, after whom we took the world
as full of hope and promise, then, like him,
as baffling when it ignored us when we called
and needed to be found where we had hid.

Our father who art somewhere now, we hope,
although we have the proof of where he is,

divided among us, in separate memories,
and things that he loved marked by his ownership.

The minutes keep repeating, each without him,
but if eternity is outside of time,
there's no time like the present to imagine him,
our father restored to memory and beyond.

In the rented bed in the sunlit sewing room,
a dusk rose from his open mouth and eyes.
It was our shadow cast as we crowded around him,
meeting his shadow still falling on all of us.

My Father Returns as a Luna Moth

My father returns as a luna moth,
a green hand under the porch light.
He comes back as a tree frog on the kitchen window
blown there by the storm overnight.

My father returns as a red wasp
and the venom she sticks in my knee.
He sleeps in a paper capsule
of the nest under the eave.

And back he comes as a file of old letters,
angry, commonplace, merry, and grim,
airmail flimsy, stationery stiff,
from him to me, me to him.

He returns as hymn tunes and cuff links,
a diamond pinky ring that won't fit.
He looks out as the passage from Micah engraved
on his columbarium niche.

"Do justice. Love kindness. Walk humbly."
He's there in a kiss with sealed lips.
He's reborn as the o-gape of his last breath,
in the solar eclipse.

One day his signs and wonders
may no longer make me think twice.
Will he ever stop returning?
Not in my life.

End of Summer

       seemed impossible.
How could there be an end to summer?
Boys and girls with blond sand on our brown necks,
when school clamped down in August, we protested,
"But it's still summer!"
                               But it wasn't.
The sun still burning, the waves still breaking,
summer always ended before it ended.
"It's not as hot this year as other summers, is it?"
she wrote as we were leaving one another.

Summer, a country like a floating memory,
the good place you can wear upon your skin
like a lace of salt or the name of one you loved.
And fall and spring and winter, for that matter.

At the end, asked which was her favorite season,
the woman who'd been born in the height of summer
looked at the window where the leaves were turning,
and answered, "All of them."

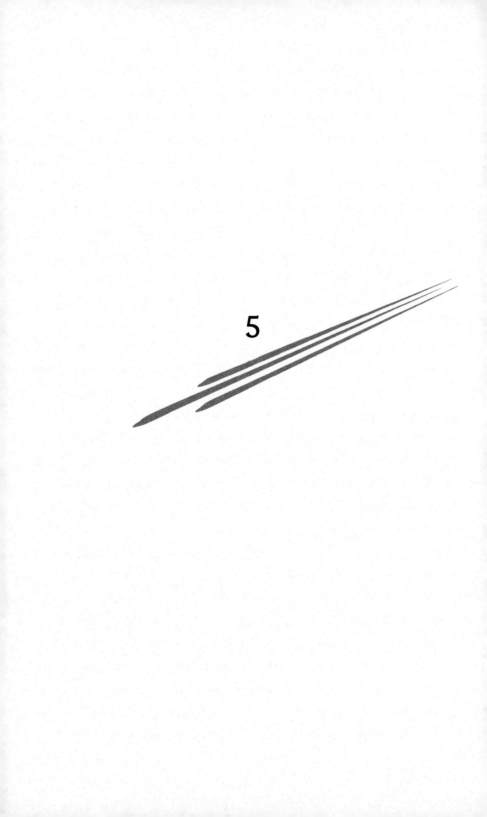

5

Overpass Ivy

I love the mountains, I love the rolling hills
Camp Song

I love the ivy dangling from the L.A. overpass,
the long ropes of dark leaves hanging still
and the tough old vines embracing the concrete pillars.
Shadows gather layering older shadows
and cars hurry beneath, people look up a moment
at the relics, as if Wordsworth's River Wye
and not the dilapidated abbey down stream
were the ruin to be cherished. I cherish the ruins
of home. The churches my father built and served
and his father, sold to new businesses,
the school yards and neighborhood backyards,
the congregations of tight-knit communities,
all treated as tear downs, purpose driven
deaths to bring forth new spaces,
new values for the soul's real estate,
new ways of traveling to a different life.
America is full of ruins, said Randall Jarrell,
the ruins of hopes. But home is a kind of hope,
and hope can be restored in memory.
Coleridge must have dreamed of the River Otter
winding in a mazy motion through his childhood
and remade it as the sacred Alph. I saw that one evening
in Ottery St. Mary, looking toward the Channel.
That need to remake already stirs
in the swollen urge crossing the Aegean
as a bombed street lives again in a bombed heart.

We will cross gulfs of space for a new foothold
that may allow us time to dream of return
in song, in story, but never in person.
Every memory of home is an origin story.
It may be Eden we miss but also before Eden,
that garden yet to be imagined, filled with lives
which will make our lives.
            The strands of overpass ivy
hang straight down, slenderer but as heavy
as Isambard Kingdom Brunel's massive chain links,
the industrial triumph now declining
in rusty stillness, the whole earth a broken
breathing, St. Stephen pelted with clods of smoke.
The weather forecast collapses like a telescope.
All that seemed so far away now fits in a palm
which we fit inside, the closing and secreting fist
of a sea anemone where the tide pool
encrusts its foundations as if a shrine
once stood there and now stands again,
inverted, its gargoyle barnacles, opening
tendrilously in hunger.
            It is always back to the sea,
and now the sea responds accepting
the invitation to rise and cleanse and undermine
itself with the poisons it will add to its home brew.
It is why we inquire of a knob of rock
catching sunlight in the Kuiper Belt
if it was from Abyssinia, Alexandria, Anaheim, the moon,
if it knew the moon and earth when they were young,
if it can speak for a particular comet carrying
water like Gunga Din to sprinkle some imperial throat
near the heart—cratered but still at work.
Ruins always tell us they were a place once.

And we dig them up, hurtling at the speed of a brush tip,
to sip dust from the imprint of a scallop shell.
    The stranded vines cling to the concrete,
a hanging garden of Babylon,
colossal wreck and local antique breakdown,
still in the windless motion below the traffic.
Perhaps they meant to pull it all down,
then saw, from another angle, the seductive cascade,
neither an invitation to nor a caution against
going up or coming down, nodding yes or nodding no,
and left it for others to notice, witness, and marvel at,
among the hills of Silver Lake, near the ancient reservoir.
Boom diada, boom diada, boom.

Acknowledgments

My thanks to the following publications, where the poems in this book first appeared: *The American Journal of Poetry, The Arkansas International, The Atlantic, Blackbird, Five Points, The Harvard Review, The Hopkins Review, The Hudson Review, Literary Imagination, Measure, Plume, Post Road Magazine, Rattle, The San Diego Reader.*

"Our Inconstant Moon" appeared in *The Inconstant Moon: Poems to the Moon*, ed. Enid Mark, the ELM Press, 2007.

"Altarpiece, Three for Dante" appeared in *Divining Dante*, eds. Paul Munden and Nessa O'Mahony, Recent Works Press, 2021.

"With Marcus Aurelius in Los Angeles" is for Ewa Hryniewicz-Yarbrough; "The Arrow Paradox" is for David Barber; "Near Cape Lookout" is for my sisters Katie Law and Luanne Jarman-Miller; "Overpass Ivy" is for Amy.

The book's epigraph is from Zbigniew Herbert's "To Marcus Aurelius," translated by Czesław Miłosz and Peter Dale Scott.

photo by Amy Jarman

Mark Jarman is the author of eleven books of poetry. *The Heronry* is his most recent. He has also published five books of essays and reviews, including *Dailiness* (Paul Dry Books, 2020), and won numerous awards for his poetry. He is Centennial Professor of English, Emeritus, at Vanderbilt University in Nashville, TN.